Within Our Reach

Obtaining the Peace and Power of the Gospel

David Martin Call

Deseret Book
Salt Lake City, Utah

Library of Congress Cataloging in Publication Data

Call, David Martin.
    Within our reach.

    Bibliography: p.
    Includes index.
    1. Christian life—Mormon authors. I. Title.
BX8656.C27 1984   248.4'8933   83-26162
ISBN 0-87747-975-5

To Vaughn P. Call, my father, and to Eunice E. Call, my mother, whose example and teachings have always stressed that the peace and power of the gospel are within our reach.

Contents

Preface

Much has been written and spoken about the difficulty of achieving righteousness and spirituality during times of relative peace and prosperity. (See Helaman 12:1-6.) Anciently during prosperous times, the prophets found it necessary to keep the minds of Church members continually upon death, hell, and the judgment to keep them stirred up in the remembrance of their duties before God. The prophet

Enos recorded, "The people of Nephi did till the land, and raise all manner of grain, and of fruit, and flocks of herds, and flocks of all manner of cattle of every kind, and goats, and wild goats, and also many horses.

"And there were exceedingly many prophets among us. And the people were a stiffnecked people, hard to understand. And there was nothing save it was exceeding harshness, preaching and prophesying of wars, and contentions, and destructions, and continually reminding them of death, and the duration of eternity, and the judgments and the power of God, and all these things—stirring them up continually to keep them in the fear of the Lord. I say there was nothing short of these things, and exceedingly great plainness of speech, would keep them from going down speedily to destruction." (Enos 1:23.)

So closely related are the prosperity of God's people and a loss of spirituality that the Book of Mormon records that at the very moment God prospers his people, they begin to forget him: "At the very time when he doth prosper his people, . . . then is the time that they do harden their hearts, and do forget the Lord their God, . . . and this because of their ease, and their exceedingly great prosperity." (Helaman 12:2.)

Finally, the chastening hand of the Lord is necessary to break the pride of the people, to bring them again to remember their Lord. "Except the Lord doth chasten his people with many afflictions, yea, except he doth visit them with death and with terror, and with famine and with all manner of pestilence, they will not remember him." (Helaman 12:3.)

In the infinite wisdom and mercy of God, for the most part we have not been visited with death, terror, famine, and all manner of pestilence, but rather have enjoyed peace, comfort, and "exceedingly great prosperity" for many years.

The Lord has largely left it up to ourselves, our leaders, our teachers, and our parents to help us remember the Lord. Our faithfulness has, in a large degree, been an individual affair, one of stirring oneself up to spiritual heights without being driven or compelled by God's chastening hand.

The tendency of the "natural man," however, is to relax, to be "lukewarm," and to not strive with all one's "heart, might, mind, and strength" in the direction of spirituality.

This book deals with the stirring up of one's own soul to greater heights of spirituality by looking to God with "full purpose of heart." (D&C 18:28.)

PART 1

Understanding Our Spiritual State

1
The Eternal Standard

What others think of us often consumes our attention at the expense of what God thinks of us. And usually what we think of ourselves depends upon whether or not we are viewed favorably by others. Foolish or not, the fact exists—we want to be friends with the world.

Having been placed upon this earth among millions of God's sons and daughters, we usually rely on each other's weaknesses to evaluate our strengths, and on each other's strengths to evaluate our weaknesses. Man is our usual standard of comparison. When we gauge our worth, abilities, popularity, or character, it is with man that we compare. If we excel, it is relative to what is considered the norm of excellence among mankind. No matter how great our successes or degrading our failures, they are all relative to our standard of comparison.

Why is mankind the usual standard of comparison? Because he is the most intelligent form of life on this planet. Certainly we cannot compare our successes and failures with those of a rabbit or a rosebush.

While we are busily comparing ourselves with others, others are busily comparing themselves with us. Our neighbor always has one eye glancing over our fence. He assesses his situation by comparing it with ours. And we return the favor by comparing our situation with his. This comparison often results in stiff competitiveness. We seem to be almost unconsciously driven to compete with others, even at the expense of truth and fair play.

As long as man is our standard of comparison, we accept his standards of living, his judgments of right and wrong, his opinions, and his philosophies—in fact, his all in all—as ours. So, if man becomes corrupt, sensual, and devilish, our standard of comparison becomes a standard of corruption. Thus, Satan can lead the great masses of mankind down to hell merely by traditionalizing them in the path of wickedness.

When we become engrossed in what the world thinks of us, we are led into error and eventually into bondage. But sooner or later we will come to realize that it is not what others think of us that is of real importance, but what

God thinks of us. This was perhaps the first hard lesson the young Prophet Joseph Smith had to learn. The Lord told him, "Behold, how oft you have transgressed the commandments and the laws of God, and have gone on in the persuasions of men. For, behold, you should not have feared man more than God." (D&C 3:6-7.) The Lord also said, "I command you, my servant Joseph, to repent and walk more uprightly before me, and to yield to the persuasions of men no more." (D&C 5:21.)

The point is clear: while the majority of mankind spend their years trying to meet the persuasions of men, the correct standard to be met is the laws of God. God, not man, should be our standard of comparison.

The Savior said, "Be ye . . . perfect, even as your Father which is in heaven is perfect." (Matthew 5:48.) And after his resurrection, he told the Nephites, "I would that ye should be perfect even as I, or your Father who is in heaven is perfect." (3 Nephi 12:48.)

We are to pattern ourselves after the Father and the Son. As they are pure, we must be pure. As they are holy, we too must seek holiness. Thus, by elevating our standard of comparison from man to God, we raise our standard from one of corruption to one of perfection.

One who seeks this standard of perfection soon reconstructs his whole way of life, his whole way of thinking, to coincide with it. "We have the mind of Christ," said the Apostle Paul to the Corinthians. (1 Corinthians 2:16.) With this "mind of Christ" we would rather be with the godlike, regardless of their situation, than to be with the ungodly in their sins—"choosing rather to suffer affliction with the people of God, than to enjoy the pleasures of sin for a season." (Hebrews 11:25.) We are also able to turn our backs on the things of this world, which only days before consumed our entire attention—"esteeming the reproach of Christ greater riches than the treasures of Egypt." (Hebrews 11:26.)

When we compare ourselves with God, competitiveness vanishes. Can the finite compete with the infinite? Can mortal compete with immortal? Can the glory of man compare with the glory of God?

When we compare ourselves with others, we may glory in our strength, superior intelligence, or wealth. But when we compare ourselves with God, we have nothing and, in comparison, are nothing. After being in the presence of God, Moses declared, "Now, for this cause I know that man is nothing, which thing I never had supposed." (Moses 1:10.)

It is not that man is worthless, without purpose or potential, but that in comparison to God's divine nature, in comparison to a Being who radiates a fulness of glory, fallen, mortal man fades into nothingness.

When we understand our relationship to God, our desire to dominate others is replaced with the desire to help others. We realize that all people are weak, in need of divine help. We become meek, humble, and submissive to the Lord.

But when we learn that we are nothing in comparison with God, what of our self-esteem? Do we lose all self-worth? Not at all. For we also learn that God is our Father and that we may become like him. Our self-esteem is enhanced by this knowledge and newfound relationship. The knowledge that we are not mere creatures of chance, who live and die and are no more, that we are of divine parentage, gives us, for the first time, divine self-esteem. Eternal worth, endless influence, everlasting joy—these concepts develop true self-esteem.

The Apostle Paul noted that "we are the offspring of God." (Acts 17:29.) Since this is true, we should measure our lives not by the standards of men but by the standards of God, for they are true and unchanging standards.

Brigham Young, Jr., said this: "Men do not look at things as God looks at them, therefore it is indispensably necessary for each individual Latter-day Saint to have the Spirit of God within him, that he may do His will and not carry out his own views. . . .

"I know it is true that God's ways are not as men's ways; and for a man to undertake to be a Latter-day Saint while groping in the dark by trusting wholly to the intelligence of his own mind, is the hardest work imaginable; it is the most laborious task that can be, for any individual on the earth to try to be what he ought to be before his God without the Holy Spirit to assist and guide him." (*Journal of Discourses* 15:140.)

We have been raised among the Gentiles and have not escaped unscathed. To a large extent, their ways have become our ways, and their thoughts have become our thoughts. We have been guilty of living in the world while being of the world. Now we must deal with the consequences. John Taylor said, "Mixed up as we have been with the Gentile world, and having formed our habits and customs among them—having been accustomed to feel as they feel, to reason as they reason, and to associate with them, it is sometimes very difficult for us to understand what would really be for our benefit and advantage, whether pertaining to this world or to the world which is to come." (*Journal of Discourses* 6:105.)

With these Gentile notions and conceptions in our hearts and minds, are we free from seeing as they see, from doing as they do? Most certainly not. We are often guilty of falling into the same snares and making the same incorrect judgments. We are even guilty at times of calling "evil good, and good evil," of putting "darkness for light, and light for darkness," of putting "bitter for sweet, and sweet for bitter." (Isaiah 5:20.)

Lorenzo Snow said, "We need assistance. We are liable to do that which will lead us into trouble and darkness, and those things which will not tend to our good, but with the assistance of that comforter which the Lord has primised his Saints, if we are careful to listen to its whisperings, and understand the nature of its language, we may avoid much trouble and serious difficulty." (*Journal of Discourses* 19:341.)

We must be aware of our vulnerability, aware that the things of this world have a powerful influence over us. The views and opinions of those around us affect us immensely. We are very susceptible to the enticings of this world, and it requires conscious effort to combat its influences.

We must "look to God and live." (Alma 37:47.) This means listening to the still, small voice rather than the voice of the world around us; it means making changes, giving up old ways for new.

The whole purpose of the gospel is to bring about change to transform us so that we can enjoy a celestial society. We must not look upon this telestial society in which we live as the norm of behavior; we must look to God.

2
The Holy Ghost—
the Measure of
Spirituality

We know that we are to measure our lives by eternal standards. But how do we do this? How do we learn of our standing before the Lord? Not through any mortal means; that is impossible. We are immortal, divine beings; therefore, the only true understanding of our worthiness must come from a divine source, from God himself!

In order to discover who we really are, what we really can become, and how we really stand in the eyes of the

Lord, we must seek the medium through which these messages are communicated. We must seek the Holy Spirit. Erastus Snow said, "If we live continually so as to enjoy the guidance of the Holy Spirit of God, it will hold the mirror before our eyes, and enable us to understand our positions before God as plainly as we behold our natural faces in the glass." (*Journal of Discourses* 13:8.)

Speaking of the power of the Holy Spirit to reveal our true nature, John Taylor said, "You have seen its effects upon us. It shall bring things past to your remembrance; it shall show you things to come; it shall make prophets of you; your sons and daughters shall see visions; the heavens shall be opened unto you; you shall know of your origin, comprehend who you are, what you are, where you are going to, the relationship which exists between you and your God; and there shall be a channel opened between the eternal worlds and you; and the purposes of God shall be made known unto you." (*Journal of Discourses* 5:243.)

Members of The Church of Jesus Christ of Latter-day Saints are not left ignorant concerning their standing in the eyes of the Lord. The Lord has given us a sure witness, a means by which we may contemplate and evaluate our standing, not yearly, but daily, hourly, every moment of our lives.

How may we know every moment of our lives? Because "the Lord hath said he dwelleth not in unholy temples, but in the hearts of the righteous doth he dwell." (Alma 34:36.)

When we are in harmony with the Holy Spirit, it is a witness that we are clean, pure, and acceptable as a residence for this divine gift. For the Spirit will not dwell in an unclean tabernacle.

If we do not enjoy the presence of the Spirit (after

receiving the gift of the Holy Ghost), what may we con-
clude? That its absence is a witness that we are out of harmony, that we are not clean, pure, and acceptable as a residence for this divine gift. Consider Heber C. Kimball's
remarks: "The Holy Ghost, being a pure Spirit or influence, even after all this is done [receiving the gift of the
Holy Ghost], will have an objection to perform his office
in an impure tabernacle. That is the reason why a great
many never receive the Holy Ghost, because they say they
are pure, and lie to God, and also to the Holy Ghost."
(*Journal of Discourses* 7:16.)

We must receive the gift of the Holy Ghost through
the proper channel, and then we must so live "that the
spirit of peace may be, not a casual visitor, but a constant
attendant,—that he may take up his abode with [us]; and
when an individual takes up his abode with [us], then [we]
do not consider him a transient visitor, but there is his
home—there is where he lodges, where he stays, where he
imparts blessings,—if he is a minister of blessings, where
he imparts good, if he has any good to impart." (Amasa
Lyman, *Journal of Discourses* 5:310.)

Brigham Young said, "The fact that we receive this
Comforter, the Holy Ghost, is proof that the spirit in war-
ring with the flesh has overcome, and by continuing in
this state of victory over our sinful bodies we become the
sons and daughters of God, Christ having made us free,
and whosoever the Son makes free is free indeed." (*Journal of Discourses* 18:259.)

So anxious is the Lord that we enjoy this knowledge
and spiritual fulfillment that he has established numerous
channels or avenues whereby we may come in contact
with the Holy Spirit and therefore be sure of our standing
in his eyes.

When we enjoy the spirit of prayer, when we truly communicate with God, is that not a witness of our standing?

When we enjoy the spirit of fasting, when we truly subject the will of the flesh to the will of the spirit and thus enjoy the presence of the Holy Ghost, is that not a witness?

When we partake of the spirit of the sacrament, renew our covenants, remember Christ's sacrifice, and enjoy the Spirit of the Lord throughout the coming week, is that not a witness?

When we worship in the temple, seek our Father in his holy house, and there partake of his Spirit, is that not a witness?

The Lord has established many channels so that we, his children, might enjoy his uplifting Spirit and be sure of our standing in his eyes—so that we may truly understand the state of our souls.

As we struggle with mortality, temptation, and our physical nature, sometimes we enjoy the companionship of the Spirit and sometimes we do not, for we are not always worthy to receive the Spirit. We vacillate between righteousness and sin.

The Lord has said, "I know thy works, that thou art neither cold nor hot: I would thou wert cold or hot. So then because thou art lukewarm, and neither cold nor hot, I will spue thee out of my mouth." (Revelation 3: 15-16.)

According to this scripture, we may be cold, lukewarm, or hot in keeping the commandments. The degree to which we enjoy the companionship of the Holy Ghost is a sure guide as to which category we are presently in.

When we feel cold toward the things of the Spirit,

when we are doubtful, confused, angry, uncaring, and depressed, the Holy Ghost is not with us. We are cold.

When we merely go through the motions of spirituality—praying, but not always with real intent; attending Church, but not always applying the gospel in our lives; fulfilling the letter but not always the spirit of our callings—sometimes the Spirit is with us and sometimes it is not. We are lukewarm.

When we live the gospel with all our hearts, not just because it is expected of us or to fill the letter of the law, we are filled with light, intelligence, happiness, truth, and power—we enjoy the companionship of the Holy Ghost. The Apostle Paul wrote, "God hath not given us the spirit of fear; but of power, and of love, and of a sound mind." (2 Timothy 1:7.) He also wrote, "The fruit of the Spirit is love, joy, peace, longsuffering, gentleness, goodness, faith, meekness, temperance." (Galatians 5:22-23.) When we feel the Spirit to this extent, we are hot.

The key to understanding our spiritual state is coming to the understanding that the Lord is telling us who we are, what we are, and where we are headed, all by means of withholding or bestowing his Spirit.

When we are out of harmony, the Spirit of the Lord is withdrawn. When we are in harmony, the Spirit is bestowed. It is simple, and it is direct. The Holy Ghost is the true measure of our spiritual state.

3
Obtaining a Lively Hope

A great many people feast upon imagination instead of feasting upon that which is tangible, and they will allow their minds to be led away by fancy, and will make out how great they will be at some future time, and how good they intend to be and how much of the Holy Ghost they expect to receive; but the idea is, what do you enjoy at the present time, and what are the blessings you enjoy at this present moment, right now? Am I doing right to-day? Is the Holy Ghost in me now? Is God's blessing with me now—(not at some other time)? If so, then all is well. (Jedediah M. Grant, *Journal of Discourses* 3:11.)

We are an imaginative and hopeful people. We hope we are on the road to eternal life. We hope the gospel is taking effect in our life. We hope our course is in accordance with God's will. We hope we will inherit the celestial kingdom. We hope our marriage was sealed by the Holy Spirit of Promise so that we might have claim on each other and on our families in the hereafter. We hope for all these things and can even imagine ourselves receiving them, but how confident are we that we will be worthy to obtain them?

The Apostle Peter spoke of having a *lively* hope of receiving eternal life. (1 Peter 1:3-4.) This is more than mere wishing. It is a hope based on the knowledge that our lives are in accordance with God's will. Merely to wish, to suppose, to imagine, to assume that our lives are acceptable to God is not enough. Joseph F. Smith, quoting from the *Lectures on Faith*, said this: "An actual knowledge to any person, that the course of life which he pursues is according to the will of God, is essentially necessary to enable him to have that confidence in God without which no person can obtain eternal life. For unless a person does know that he is walking according to the will of God, it would be an insult to the dignity of the Creator were he to say that he would be a partaker of his glory when he should be done with the things of this life. But when he has this knowledge, and most assuredly knows that he is doing the will of God, his confidence can be equally strong that he will be a partaker of the glory of God." (*Journal of Discourses* 19:23; see *Lectures on Faith*, p. 33.)

The Spirit of the Lord is such that it enables us to see ourselves "as the Lord sees" us. (John Taylor, *Journal of Discourses* 6:166.) A true soul analysis can be made; we can and must know of our standing in the Lord's eyes.

This requires a great deal of honesty. We must be willing to see our spiritual state for what it really is and not shirk it off as being unknowable. We must think, "I have received the gospel and its ordinances. I have been promised through my confirmation of receiving the unspeakable gift of the Holy Ghost. I have been instructed sufficiently as to how I should obtain the Spirit of the Lord, from personal prayer to temple worship. Now, how is it with me?"

Jedediah M. Grant asked, "What are the blessings you enjoy at the present moment, right now?" (*Journal of Discourses* 3:11.) And he said, "I wish to enquire whether the channel is open between you and the heavens, and do you draw daily from that source? If so, then you are in the narrow path, and rejoicing in the truth." (*Journal of Discourses* 3:10.)

But if not, what does it mean? What are the implications? Where does it leave us? Are we lost and hopeless?

The scriptures declare that "signs shall follow them that believe." (D&C 84:65.) But when they don't, when one does not enjoy the gifts of the Spirit, what does that imply?

Consider another disturbing question: "I ask of you, my brethren of the church, have ye spiritually been born of God? Have ye received his image in your countenances? Have ye experienced this mighty change in your hearts?" (Alma 5:14.)

Consider still another issue. When you were immersed in the waters of baptism, you received half of your baptism. Have you received the other half? Have you been baptized with fire and the Holy Ghost?

Joseph Smith declared, "Baptism by water is but half

a baptism, and is good for nothing, without the other half—that is, the baptism of the Holy Ghost." (*Teachings of the Prophet Joseph Smith*, p. 314.)

Consider Lorenzo Snow's baptism of the Holy Ghost just two or three weeks after his confirmation: "I heard a sound, just above my head, like the rustling of silken robes, and immediately the Spirit of God descended upon me, completely enveloping my whole person, filling me, from the crown of my head to the soles of my feet, and O, the joy and happiness I felt! No language can describe the almost instantaneous transition from a dense cloud of mental and spiritual darkness into a refulgence of light and knowledge, as it was at that time imparted to my under-standing. I then received a perfect knowledge that God lives, that Jesus Christ is the Son of God, and of the restoration of the holy Priesthood, and the fulness of the Gospel.

"It was a complete baptism—a tangible immersion in the heavenly principle or element, the Holy Ghost; and even more real and physical in its effects upon every part of my system than the immersion by water. . . . I cannot tell how long I remained in the full flow of the blissful enjoyment and divine enlightenment, but it was several minutes before the celestial element which filled and sur-rounded me began gradually to withdraw." (Eliza R. Snow, *Biography and Family Record of Lorenzo Snow*, pp. 7-9.)

Have you received such a baptism of fire?

These are soul-searching questions. They hurt, they sting, and they make us uncomfortable. It is much easier to avoid such questions than it is to face them, but face them we must!

Let us search our souls. Let us so live that we might

obtain a "lively hope," one that is founded in truth, one that will give us confidence, even boldness, in the presence of God. We cannot and must not settle for anything less.

PART 2

Uncovering
the Cause
of Our Misery

4

Spiritual Dissatisfaction

Once we have honestly examined our spiritual state, using the presence or absence of the Holy Spirit as the basis for our conclusion, we may discover that we are only lukewarm in living the gospel. We realize that this is the true cause of most of our problems, of our despondency, of our spiritual weakness. We realize that we are spiritually dissatisfied.

Were it possible for us in this state to stand and bear

our true testimony, it might sound something like this: "It is my testimony that God can be found, but I have grown weary of hearing, reading, and pondering other's successes without having success myself.

"I am weary of reading of Nephi being caught away in the Spirit to an exceedingly high mountain and receiving the desires of his heart (1 Nephi 11:1), and of the brother of Jared, who had such faith that the Lord could not withhold himself from him. (Ether 3:9.)

"I am weary of reading about the Kirtland Temple manifestations, where the Spirit of the Lord rushed down upon the temple and filled it as if with cloven tongues of fire, and of Joseph Smith walking the banks of the Mississippi River, healing the sick as he went. And of Lorenzo Snow, who, just two weeks after his baptism of water, received a baptism of fire and of the Holy Ghost.

"Can I not experience these things for myself? Are the heavens closed to me? Have my prayers become 'as sounding brass, or a tinkling cymbal'? (1 Corinthians 13:1.) O God, where art thou? And what is the cause of my 'lukewarmness' and my soul misery?"

In answer to our plea, the Lord might open to us Lehi's vision of the tree of life (1 Nephi 8:2-36), but from a special point of view. Let us see what that vision might be like.

The vision opens:

I see the rod of iron and feel the river of filthiness running alongside it. I am in the river, within arms' distance of the rod. The river does not seem filthy, only swift.

I sense that I have been in these waters for years and that I have discovered over the years that I could offset the current by

steadily swimming upstream. Although I might be only swimming in place, I have always taken pride in the fact that I am not carried downstream by the swiftness of the current.

I even feel a sense of security; the rod is near, and has been near most of my life. I have kept close to it, close enough that when the time comes to meet my Savior, I can grab hold. I have been careful about that.

In the past, the Spirit has sometimes urged me to reach for the rod, even jump for it, if possible, but being so close I cannot see the urgency to do so.

Suddenly things change. The Savior is here! He is hurrying the Saints who were prepared along the rod, ushering them into his bridal chamber. They move rapidly. There is an air of excitement and anticipation.

I have prepared for this moment all my life; it is time to move. All I have to do is reach, reach for the rod and make my way into the bridal chamber before the door closes.

I reach, but to do so I must stop swimming, and the river takes me farther from the rod than I was before. I panic. For the first time I realize that having the rod so close was no guarantee that I would be able to grasp it in my hour of need. Why didn't I listen to the promptings of the Spirit? There is not enough time to reach the rod now.

I see the Saints who were prepared passing in front of me, within arms' distance of me. Why don't they reach out and help me? They seem to be looking at something of great importance just ahead of them. They clutch the rod with both hands, and in this moment of urgency not one of them dares let go, not even with one hand, to help me.

I see others passing behind me, being carried rapidly downstream by the current. They call to me, they plead for help, but they are quickly gone. I must continue thrashing to-

ward the rod. I must not concern myself with those poor souls, for I cannot help them; I am in danger of being carried away myself.

Everything is happening so swiftly. The people seem to be keenly aware of the tragedies all around them and of their inability to help at this crucial moment. Yes, all seem aware of their own position, of having to stand on their own.

I begin to see things as they really are. I see my own desperate straits, my helplessness, my carelessness. I had thought there would be no difficulty in grasping the rod. I was always so close, so comfortably close, that I never tried.

The doors! The doors of the bridal chamber are closing. This can't be happening. This can't be true. O Lord God Almighty, don't let it be true!

The doors close.

I'm stunned, staring and motionless, and the current moves me out into deeper water.

I fix my eyes on those doors, on all that I hoped for, on all that I supposed and imagined would be mine. The river moves heedlessly on as I sink into its dark and filthy depths.

The vision closes.

5

Between
Two Worlds

Many who are lukewarm are puzzled by the gospel. It appears to be two things at once: the way to happiness and the cause of their unhappiness. Something is wrong, but what? Daniel H. Wells said, "Many a soul may be drooping for the want of spiritual moisture, and they do not know what the difficulty is. There are obstacles in the way that need removing, that our minds may be enlightened by the light of the

Spirit of the living God." (*Journal of Discourses* 12:234.)

Wilford Woodruff said this: "If I do not enjoy the Holy Spirit, there is something the matter, and I should labour until that is removed, for I consider that to be the first turning key, and we should do this to prove that we are honest before the Lord, and that we desire to do right in our minds and in our hearts." (*Journal of Discourses* 4:191.)

How many more years will we spend learning the lesson that, as Brigham Young said, "without the light of the Spirit of Christ, no person can truly enjoy life." (*Journal of Discourses* 8:66.)

We attend our meetings, pay our tithing, and all other things as we are required, and yet many of us still seem to be miserable. We do not really enjoy our religion. Something seems missing; something is definitely wrong.

As long as we do not enjoy the Spirit of the Lord, as long as that Spirit is not part of our lives, we remain in this miserable, discontented, and disturbed state. Brigham Young asked, "Is it not a hard task to live this religion without enjoying the spirit of it? Such a course worries the feelings, fills a person with sorrow and affliction, and makes him miserable. . . . How is it with you who do not enjoy the spirit of your religion? It is a hard life for you to live." (*Journal of Discourses* 8:198.)

Many of us are not happy, but it is not the gospel's fault. We sense that, and we know it. But, as Brigham Young said, "we wish it was some way else; we wish our circumstances were different; we are not happy; something or the other is always wrong; we wish to do just right, but we are very unhappy. I desire to tell you that your own conduct is the cause of all this.

"'But,' says one, 'I have done nothing wrong, nothing evil.'

"No matter whether you have or not, you have given way to a spirit of temptation. There is not a man or woman in this congregation, or on the face of the earth, that has the privilege of the holy Gospel, and lives strictly to it, whom all hell can make unhappy. You cannot make the man, woman, or child unhappy, who possesses the Spirit of the living God; unhappiness is caused by some other spirit." (*Journal of Discourses* 3:343.)

Why is it that we do not have the companionship of the Holy Ghost, that member of the Godhead who would bring us knowledge, power, and happiness?

The vision of the iron rod and the filthy river points out the real problem. The lukewarm Saint sees no reason to leave the filthy river, to repent of all his sins. After all, he thinks, there is plenty of time for that. But he is careful never to get too far from the iron rod, the word of God, for he knows that the day will come when he will need to grasp it firmly and pull himself from the river to meet the Lord. But in the meantime, he refuses to choose one over the other. He is caught between two worlds.

We enjoy this life and the things of this world. On the other hand, we desire to enjoy the life the gospel has to offer and the things of the heavenly world. But the Lord has repeatedly told us that we cannot have both worlds: "He that loveth his life shall lose it; and he that hateth his life in this world shall keep it unto life eternal." (John 12:25) And again, "No man can serve two masters: for either he will hate the one, and love the other; or else he will hold to the one, and despise the other. Ye cannot serve God and mammon." (Matthew 6:24.)

Regardless of the Lord's warning, many of us find ourselves trying to hold on to the best of both worlds, and yet we end up enjoying the best of neither.

Orson Pratt described the problem well: "We oftentimes deprive ourselves of the blessings and enjoyments which we might receive, through the darkness of our minds, through our selfishness, through our neglect of keeping the commandments of God, through our disobedience, and through the abundance of cares and perplexities with which we have to contend in this mortal existence. All these things have a tendency, more or less, to darken the understanding and drive away from the heart that peaceable Spirit which whispers peace to the minds of the sons and daughters of God. I often reflect upon this subject much, and inquire in my own mind, and try to search out some of the causes of our being so far beneath the privileges which are guaranteed to us in the Gospel of Jesus Christ. It is not because the promises of God have failed. It is not because we are not worshipping the same Being whom the Saints worshipped in ancient days. It is not because there are insurmountable obstacles in our way; but the cause lies in our own selves. We are the individuals that shut out this light of heaven—this light of truth that would otherwise shine upon our understandings." (*Journal of Discourses* 7:308.)

Many of our nonmember friends and neighbors seem to enjoy their lives, and our member friends and neighbors who have developed the Spirit of the Lord in their lives seem to enjoy theirs. On both sides, everyone seems to enjoy life but us. But why?

Every soul who is given a testimony of the gospel is given a cross to bear. The cross was given to us for a specific purpose—that we might crucify the "man of sin" within us:

And they that are Christ's have crucified the flesh with the affections and lusts. (Galatians 5:24.)

Knowing this, that our old man is crucified with him, that the body of sin might be destroyed, that henceforth we should not serve sin. (Romans 6:6.)

He that will not bear his cross for Christ's sake is not worthy to be called a Saint, nor will he ever become one: "And whosoever doth not bear his cross, and come after me, cannot be my disciple." (Luke 14:26.)

Because of our testimonies, we have taken up the cross. Our testimonies have, in a sense, nailed us to it. There are, however, two ways to come down from this cross.

One way is to deny our testimonies. One who denies his testimony is free to come down from the cross and go about his earthly business. This, of course, would deny him any hope of eternal life and place him under greater condemnation than if he had never heard the gospel.

The only other way to come down from the cross is to put to death the "natural man" within us. (Mosiah 3:19.) Once we have accomplished this, we are taken from the cross and buried with Christ. We then come forth out of the grave a new creature; we have been spiritually reborn.

To those of us who cannot deny our testimonies and yet have not been willing to crucify unto death the "natural man" is left the only other alternative—to remain hanging on the cross.

From this vantage point, we see both worlds: the earthly world below us, with its pleasantries, and the heavenly world above us, with its promises and assurance. Either world seems to have its advantage over our present predicament: unfortunately, we want both.

The Savior does not want us to hang on the cross

needlessly. He himself knew when it was time to say, "It is finished." (John 19:30.) He had a greater work to perform. So do we. But as long as we remain upon the cross, we are unable to perform our greater work. The Savior needs saints who have put to death the "natural man" and have risen with him to a "newness of life" (Romans 6:4). He needs saints who are not fixed nor stationary, but who have become living extensions of the will of the Father by overcoming the things of this world.

Yet, unwilling to completely give up the things of the world, we sentence ourselves to the needless unhappiness of hanging on to the cross.

We sometimes have a tendency to blame our testimony or the gospel itself for our miserable situation. At such times, we reason, "Wouldn't it be wonderful if I could be like the nonmember who has not yet received the gospel or heard of Joseph Smith. Then I would be happy. Then I would be free to enjoy life. Of course, I would eventually receive the gospel and exaltation, but at some later time, *after* I have enjoyed the things of this world."

We reason further, "If only I didn't know about the law of tithing. Think of how much more money I would have and what I could buy. If I didn't know about the Word of Wisdom, perhaps a good party now and then would liven things up for me. If I didn't have church every Sunday, I could have a two-day weekend instead of one.

"But I know about tithing, so I have no choice but to pay; otherwise, I couldn't live with myself. I know about the Word of Wisdom, so no lively parties for me; and besides, if I did go, someone might see me. I know about keeping the Sabbath day holy, so I'll never have a two-day weekend, and I just can't do much when I have to be back by Sunday."

Is it any wonder many of us are so miserable? Is it any wonder we are devoid of the Spirit? Is it any wonder the Savior wants to spew us out of his mouth? (Revelation 3:15-16.)

We selfishly desire the best of two worlds, and sometimes we hang onto this selfishness throughout our miserable lives. Soon, we find ourselves questioning whether the gospel really does have anything to offer us. We lose confidence in our ability to achieve spiritual fulfillment. We pay our tithing that the windows of heaven might be opened, but somehow they remain shut. We live the Word of Wisdom, and our smoking neighbor runs jubilantly past us in the park. We partake of the sacrament but do not enjoy the promised Spirit throughout the coming week. We attend to all our duties and yet remain empty. Why? Because we do not give our whole hearts to the Lord. We say to Satan, "Get thee behind me, but not too far." Brigham Young described the outcome of such a course: "Persons must so live that they can enjoy the light of the Holy Spirit, or they will have no confidence in themselves, in their religion, or in their God, and will sooner or later turn from the faith. They are in sorrow, and leave in search of something that will satisfy their minds." (*Journal of Discourses* 8:65.)

But in the meantime, because of our selfish desires, we remain hanging on the cross. Wanting the best of both worlds, we end up enjoying neither.

6

Creatures of Our Own Creation

[President Jedediah M. Grant] said that after he came back [from a visit to the spirit world] he could look upon his family and see the spirit that was in them, and the darkness that was in them; and that he conversed with them about the Gospel, and what they should do, and they replied, "Well, brother Grant, perhaps it is so, and perhaps it is not," and said that was the state of this people, to a great extent, for many are full of darkness and will not believe me. (Heber C. Kimball, *Journal of Discourses* 4:135.)

Our spiritual state cannot be treated with indifference. We must not be guilty of saying, "Perhaps I am worthy, or perhaps I am not." John Taylor said, "We are all aiming at celestial glory. Don't you know we are? We are talking about it, and we talk about being kings and priests unto the Lord; we talk about being queens and priestesses; and we talk, when we get on our high-heeled shoes, about possessing thrones, principalities, powers, and dominions in the eternal worlds, when at the same time many of us do not know how to conduct ourselves any better than a donkey does." (*Journal of Discourses* 6:166.)

God knows who we are, what we are, and what we are up to. He knows our desires, what we yearn for, the secrets of our hearts. He knows our weaknesses, our strengths, and where we are heading.

But we are creatures of our own creation. We are personally responsible for our spiritual state. We can ignore this state, or we can acknowledge it and set out to improve it.

We can treat the state of our souls with indifference. We can continue our course of unhappiness and dissatisfaction. We can hang on the cross needlessly, even endlessly, as far as mortality is concerned. But sooner or later we must place ourselves in harmony with the Spirit of the Lord. If we are wise, we will do so before it is "everlastingly too late." (Helaman 13:38.)

We must search our souls; we must search out the reasons for our unhappiness, our lack of spiritual fulfillment and enjoyment. Then we must do something about it. It does no good to whine and whimper and make excuses for the darkness inside us. The gospel was not given to us to be a cloak of self-pity but to be the very means by which we purge ourselves of this darkness.

Many of us have made bad choices that have resulted in unhappiness. Let us examine our souls and make new choices, choices that will bring the desired results—spiritual life.

The root of our unhappiness is our unwillingness to unconditionally surrender our souls to God. Yet, if it is any consolation, we are no more willing to sell our souls to the devil. We are unwilling to do either, and we live within the personal boundaries we have set.

In short, we are willing to reach only so high and to stoop only so low. We have drawn the line, set the boundaries, fixed the limits. We will give ourselves to God, but only to a certain degree—perhaps a third of our soul, or even two-thirds, but not all.

Likewise, we unwittingly give ourselves to the devil. But again, we are careful that he does not possess any more of our soul than we are willing to allot. When we feel we have reached the "bottom line," that we can sink no further, that this is the absolute limit of wickedness or darkness we will allow ourselves, we stop and we stoop no further.

These upper and lower boundaries, which we have set, form the framework in which we live. All our experiences, struggles, efforts, joys, and fears—in short, our all—are found in the boundaries we have set for ourselves.

By staying within these fixed boundaries, we are able, to a limited degree, to fluctuate between the spiritual and material worlds. Sometimes we enjoy the things of the Spirit, and sometimes we fall back into the things of the world. We are torn between the two. Our course looks something like this:

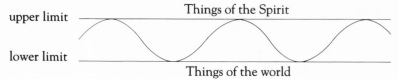

upper limit — Things of the Spirit

lower limit — Things of the world

God did not design such a course, for this course leads nowhere. Yet it is the course that many of us follow.

Is it not time we break through that upper barrier and surrender our souls to God? In our doubts and fears, we cry out "Not yet, not quite yet; in a little while, perhaps, but not yet." But *now* is the time to surrender our souls to God, to gain that inner peace and spiritual communion that we so desperately yearn for. (See Alma 34:31-32.)

Brigham Young stated it this way: "Again, I can charge you with what you will plead guilty of, if you would confess the truth, viz., you dare not quite give up all your hearts to God, and become sanctified throughout, and be led by the Holy Ghost from morning until evening, and from one year's end to another. I know this is so, and yet few will acknowledge it. I know this feeling is in your hearts, as well as I know the sun shines. . . .

"If I were to ask you individually, if you wished to be sanctified throughout, and become as pure and holy as you possibly could live, every person would say yes; yet if the Lord Almighty should give a revelation instructing you to be given wholly up to Him, and to His cause, you would shrink, saying, "I am afraid he will take away some of my darlings." That is the difficulty with the majority of this people.

"It is for you and I to wage war with that principle until it is overcome in us, then we shall not entail it upon our children." (*Journal of Discourses* 2:134.)

Yes, we are afraid. But afraid of what? We think, "If I surrender my soul to God what will become of me? What will become of my passions and appetites? Will I have to give them all up? And what about hunting and fishing? If I become a "new creature" in Christ, will I lose my desire for these things? Will I still like golfing? And what of NFL football? What of a million and one little things that I enjoy so much? Will they all be lost? Will I never enjoy them again?"

We are afraid of the unknown. We are afraid that we might be giving up a better life than we will receive. This is why we fix a limit on our spiritual fulfillment.

It may seem unreasonable, incomprehensible, even ridiculous for Latter-day Saints to fear too much of the Holy Spirit. Yet, when it jeopardizes our desire for the things of this world, it becomes a threat to worldliness, to our earthly natures; therefore, many of us fear it.

Isn't it time we overcome this unconscious fear? Why do we fear the Holy Spirit, anyway? Brigham Young said about the Holy Ghost, "It will never hurt you, but will give life, joy, peace, satisfaction, and contentment; it is light, intelligence, strength, power, glory, wisdom, and finally, it comprehends the kingdoms that are, that were, or that will be, and all that we can contemplate or desire, and will lead us to everlasting life." (*Journal of Discourses* 11:329.)

Why do we think it is a hard thing the Lord expects of us? Brigham Young explained, "The easiest life to live, by any mortal being on the earth, is to live in the light of God's countenance, and have fellowship with his Son, Jesus Christ. I know this by my own experience. In this course there is no darkness, no sorrow, no grief. The power of the Spirit of God has preserved me in the vigor of youth, and I am as active as a boy. How is it with you who do not enjoy the spirit of your religion? It is a hard life for you to live; and you had better, from this day, take a course to enjoy the Spirit of the Lord; then you will be numbered with the wise." (*Journal of Discourses* 8:198.)

We do not purposely try to avoid happiness or

spiritual fulfillment, but many of us do not enjoy them. We will never achieve spiritual fulfillment without unconditionally surrendering our souls to God; there is no other way. Brigham Young said, "All people desire to be happy. You cannot find an individual that does not wish comfort and ease. You can obtain happiness in no other way than by unreservedly submitting yourselves to your God. Let him lead us through paths of affliction and cause suffering and trouble to come upon us, still there is that consolation and comfort within that the world cannot give nor take away. That is the only solid comfort there is in this life." (*Journal of Discourses* 7:159.)

Those who are unwilling to make the required sacrifice shall have their reward in the eternal worlds, enjoying only "that which they are willing to receive, because they were not willing to enjoy that which they might have received." (D&C 88:32.)

But those who are willing, with the Lord's help, to make the required sacrifice, shall find a special place in the celestial world, a place where they enjoy that which our Father has promised all those who overcome their earthly natures—eternal life.

We are creatures of our own creation. If we are found hanging between the best of two worlds, desiring both earthly enjoyment and heavenly fulfillment, it is because we have not made up our minds as to which we desire most. But the decision is still before us, and the proper choice may still be made. It is ultimately up to us.

PART 3

The Mighty Change

7

More than a Testimony

Was Joseph Smith a prophet of God? Is the Book of Mormon the word of God? Is The Church of Jesus Christ of Latter-day Saints the only true church upon the face of the earth? Is it headed by a true and living prophet?

Someone investigating the Church has only two or three weeks to answer these important questions. In this short time, he must make an eternal decision: Is the gospel as presented by the missionaries of The Church of Jesus Christ of Latter-day Saints true or not?

If he does not respond in the affirmative, the missionaries quickly move on to another more receptive family. Unfair? Not at all. The Apostle Paul wrote, "For our gospel came not unto you in word only, but also in power, and in the Holy Ghost, and in much assurance." (1 Thessalonians 1:5.)

Thousands upon thousands have realized the truthfulness of the gospel in only two or three weeks. In that short time, they have had enough internal and external evidences to decide.

Since we can receive a testimony in such a short time, what excuse can we conjure up for spending a lifetime upon this issue? We worry and we fret over our testimonies. No matter how many witnesses we have of the truthfulness of the gospel (upon examination we would discover we have had a lifetime full of them), we seek more. We are never satisfied with what we have received, but we continually quiz ourselves: "Is the Gospel true? Yes, I do know that it is true. But do I really know it is true? Well, yes, I would have to say that I really do know. But do I really, really know? Well, yes, I would have to say that I really, really do know. But do I really, really, really know?" And so on.

Instead of being satisfied with knowing the gospel is true and getting on with the objectives of the gospel, many of us spend our time wondering if we really, really, really know of its truthfulness. What we really, really, really want is an all-encompassing sure witness. The fact that we have already had a lifetime of sure witnesses doesn't seem to satisfy us.

Is gaining a sure testimony of the truthfulness of the gospel the ultimate objective of that gospel? If it were, would we not be mightily disappointed in it? The gospel has more to offer us, much more! But many of us settle for very little of it by continuing with the tesimony issue.

Imagine yourself dying and passing behind the veil. Imagine greeting the Saints there and proudly announcing, "The gospel of Jesus Christ is true. I have that testimony, and I held on to it until the very day I died!"

Puzzled by your announcement, they might well reply, "Why, certainly the gospel of Jesus Christ is true. Is that all you have to report? Do you not know that 'the devils also believe and tremble?' Have you not discovered any more than they?"

The gospel *is* true, and we know it. Isn't it time that we get on with a greater and more important issue? "Behold, I ask of you, my brethren of the Church, have ye spiritually been born of God? Have ye received his image in your countenances? Have ye experienced this mighty change in your hearts?" (Alma 5:14.)

This spiritual rebirth is the real issue. It is the issue we have been avoiding by centering our attention upon whether or not we really, really, really have a testimony.

The fact that we have been willing to remain hanging on the cross, to remain in misery between two worlds, is sufficient evidence that we really, really, really have a testimony. Otherwise, we would have long ago come down from that cross and enjoyed the things of this world. Our problem does not come from not having a testimony but paradoxically from having one, for we refuse to go on in the gospel and be spiritually reborn: "Marvel not that all mankind, yea, men and women, all nations, kindreds, tongues and people, must be born again; yea, born of God, changed from their carnal and fallen state, to a state of righteousness, being redeemed of God, becoming his sons and daughters." (Mosiah 27:25.)

Consider this conversation between the Lord and ourselves:

"Have ye spiritually been born of God?"

"Well, I have been baptized and received the gift of the Holy Ghost by the laying on of hands, if that is what you mean."

"Have ye spiritually been born of God?"

"Well, I know the gospel is true, and I attend to all my duties. I am doing the best I can. If that qualifies me, then I guess I have been."

"Have ye spiritually been born of God?"

"Well, I'm not perfect; nobody is perfect. We are all struggling. Isn't this spiritual rebirth a process rather than an event? If so, I guess I am in the process of being spiritually reborn every day of my life."

"Have ye spiritually been born of God?"

"Well, I guess it depends on what *you* mean by being spiritually reborn."

One who does not know whether he has been spiritually reborn can be assured that he has not. Can you imagine being spiritually reborn and not knowing it? Can you imagine becoming a new creature in Christ and being unaware of it? Can you imagine experiencing a *mighty* change in your heart and yet being oblivious to this change? Can we receive Christ's image in our countenances and yet be unmindful of it?

"Have ye spiritually been born of God?" We all want to respond yes, but many of us know better.

Suppose you have been spiritually reborn. Suppose you have become a new creature in Christ. Suppose this mighty change has taken place in your heart. Is it everything you thought it would be? Are you satisfied? Do you feel or think any differently?

Many of us would be greatly disappointed were we to discover that this rebirth had, in fact, already taken place in us. We would be very dissatisfied with this mighty change, for right now we do not feel as if this mighty change had taken place.

We must not be satisfied with this. We must hunger and thirst for something greater, a more effectual creation, that creation promised those who overcome the things of this world—to become a new creature in Christ! Brigham Young said this: "I know that it may be said, and with great propriety, 'Why, my brother, we can not be sanctified in one day, we cannot overcome every evil and every passion in one day.' That is true, but this holy desire can dwell in the heart of every individual from the time that he or she is convinced that God reigns, that he is establishing his kingdom on the earth, that Jesus is our Savior, that the holy gospel has presented to us the way of life and salvation, and we believe it and can receive it with our whole hearts—I say we can have the holy and pure desire from that moment to the end of our lives, and in possessing this we have faith and favor before the Lord, and his grace is with us by the power of his Holy Spirit, and by this we can overcome temptations as we meet them. This is my experience, that is pretty good proof, is it not?" (*Journal of Discourses* 16:27.)

Many look upon spiritual rebirth as an event; others view it as an "on-going process." But if we must have a viewpoint, let it be that spiritual rebirth is an "eventful, on-going process."

When this "on-going process" becomes uneventful (we are not aware of any changes, transformations, or reformations in our lives), we may rest assured that something is wrong. When we enjoy the the Spirit of the Lord, and it leads, guides, and inspires us, our lives are eventful.

For many, this "on-going process" might more aptly be called a "going-on process," a process that seems to be going on and on to no avail. We have been baptized, received the gift of the Holy Ghost, attend the temple, and fulfill our other duties, but we must also enjoy the power associated with these avenues; we need the Holy Spirit to be part of our lives. John Taylor said, "It is not enough then, that we are baptised and have hands laid upon us for the gift of the Holy Ghost. It is not enough even that we go further than this, and receive our washing and our anointings, but that we daily and hourly and all the time live up to our religion, cultivate the Spirit of God, and have it continually with us 'as a well of water springing up unto everlasting life,' unfolding, developing, making manifest the purposes and designs of God unto us, that we may be enabled to walk worthy of the high avocation whereunto we are called, as sons and daughters of God to whom he has committed the principles of eternal truth and the oracles of God in these last days." (*Journal of Discourses* 6:106-7.)

This "eventful on-going process" of character refinement and spiritual enlightenment is called progression. Those of us who wonder if we have been spiritually reborn or not will also notice our inability to distinguish whether or not we are progressing.

Am I progressing? Am I becoming more Godlike? Again, we find ourselves avoiding such questions.

The wheel of progression is powered by the Holy Spirit. When that Spirit is absent or barely with us, we at that moment cease to progress as we should. Orson Pratt said, "Without this spirit, without revelation from the Most High, it is utterly impossible for the human family to be saved in the celestial kingdom of our Father and God." (*Journal of Discourses* 21:256-57.)

How does the wheel of progression operate? How may we know if it is turning for us? Consider this.

Sin might be broadly defined as things we do that we shouldn't do, or things we don't do that we should. And we might categorize our sins as greater sins, lesser sins, and sins of ignorance.

Our greater sins are those that trouble us most. They are the faults and failing that are uppermost in our minds and that we consider our greatest obstacles to progression.

Our lesser sins are those we know about but that we usually treat with indifference because they seem so insignificant compared to our greater sins. We often do not consider them as serious obstacles.

Sins of ignorance are sins we commit unknowingly. (See Numbers 15:27-28; Mosiah 3:11.) They are sins that we are unaware of, parts of our character that need correcting but that go unnoticed.

Each person, depending on his spiritual development, will fill in these categories with different sins. What one may consider a greater sin may be considered a lesser sin by another. One who has progressed much further than others may find himself working on problems that others would not even consider as sins.

With the aid of the Holy Spirit and the principles and ordinances of the gospel, we are able to overcome our greater sins. This is *eventful*. We know of our successes and rejoice over it. We are progressing, and we know it.

Are we progressing? Yes, most assuredly! With this victory over our greater sins, we enjoy another great event—we receive the Spirit of the Lord in a greater degree. This also is noticeable.

Therefore, we notice two experiences in our spiritual refinement: (1) a sin is overcome, and (2) the Spirit of the Lord is enjoyed to a greater degree than before. The wheel of progression has begun turning.

Next our attention is drawn to our lesser sins. These lesser sins have gained in significance; they have become our greater ones.

With this moving of our lesser sins into the greater category, we find a vacancy in our lesser-sin category. This is filled by the Holy Ghost awakening our spiritual senses to those sins we had never before even considered. Thus, the wheel of progress begins to turn.

John Taylor explained, "The light of the Holy Ghost makes manifest men's deeds, and the Spirit of God is like a 'two-edged sword, dividing the joints and the marrow,' breaking, severing, cutting, piercing, penetrating, developing, and unfolding principles that we are almost entirely ignorant of, until they come to be developed. . . . When the Spirit of the living God was poured out more copiously upon you, it developed principles that were latent within you. That Spirit enables you to see yourselves as the Lord sees you." (*Journal of Discourses* 6:166.)

This wheel of progression, this spiritual progress, can continue until we become like God. The time will come when we will no longer work on our sins but on principles and powers that have remained latent within us. The sooner we overcome our sins, the sooner we are capable of working on these principles and powers.

Yes, the gospel is *eventful*; it is effectual; it is the power of God unto salvation.

Without the Spirit of the Lord we are in danger. We are not able to make correct judgments. We learn to look upon sin with allowance. In this case, the wheel of progression reverses itself, and the process leads to destruction. Joseph F. Smith said, "Without the aid of the Holy Spirit no mortal can walk in the straight and narrow way, being unable to discern right from wrong, the genuine from the counterfeit, so nearly alike can they be made to appear. Therefore it behooves the Latter-day Saints to live pure and upright, in order that this Spirit may abide in them; for it is only possessed on the principles of righteousness." (*Journal of Discourses* 18:275.)

But if we do not live so as to have the Spirit, our greater sins are overcome by still greater ones. Our conscience becomes seared as with a hot iron, and we do not look upon our lesser sins as sins at all. This retrogression continues until it stops or until we are swallowed up in wickedness. During the entire process, the Spirit is grieved and withdraws accordingly.

The lukewarm Saint is unsure of himself. He has received a lukewarm degree of the Spirit, but is this because the wheel is moving ever so slowly forward, or is it because it is moving ever so slowly backward? Perhaps he feels himself moving forward half a turn and then back half a turn. This certainly would give him that "swimming in place" feeling. He overcomes a weakness and feels joy only to be disappointed when it creeps upon him once again. Has he met his match? Continually he overcomes it only to have it return to him. This is what drives him to the point of declaring, "I am what I am, and there's nothing I or anyone else can do about it," thus avoiding the gospel altogether.

Many of us are not satisfied with ourselves or with the gospel. The gospel, through our own apathy, has become uneventful and ineffectual in our lives, and yet we avoid facing up to this. We avoid our feeling that something is wrong, and we therefore unconsciously set the gospel of Jesus Christ aside as a thing of naught.

We have no excuse for this. The gospel is here, the priesthood is here, the Holy Spirit is available; all this is within our reach. Wilford Woodruff said, "Man possesses a spirit that must endure forever—a spirit that comes from God; and inasmuch as he is not fed from that same source or power that created him, he is not and cannot be satisfied. . . . But in these days, when the holy Priesthood is restored to us, we have no excuse for saying that our minds are not satisfied, for the blessings are given to us; they are within our reach, and it is your privilege and mine to enjoy them." (*Journal of Discourses* 8:268-69.)

8

With Full Purpose of Heart

Without a full purpose of heart, our vision becomes narrow and restricted, and our lives become little more than an account book, where good is good only because it will be placed on our credit ledger, and where bad is bad only because it will be placed on our debit ledger.

With this attitude, we view the judgment as the great day of "accounting" when the ledger sheets will be balanced out and the result will show our earnings for eternity, whether they be celestial, terrestrial, or telestial.

Of course, the scriptures do declare that we will be judged according to our works and that we should store up good deeds unto the judgment day. But we are not to do so selfishly or grudgingly, but with a genuine desire to serve the Lord and others: "Behold, if a man being evil giveth a gift, he doeth it grudgingly; wherefore it is counted unto him the same as if he had retained the gift; wherefore he is counted evil before God." (Moroni 7:8.)

Often we take food to a needy neighbor or lend a helping hand in some other way but not really wanting to do so, doing so only so we can say that we have another good deed saved up for the judgment day.

When we live in this manner, is it any wonder we are discontented and unsatisfied? Can you understand why we would not *enjoy* the gospel, why we would feel empty no matter how many good deeds we had performed?

The happiness, spiritual fulfillment, and inner peace that come from living the gospel begin with "being good," not just "doing good." A person who is "being good" is also "doing good," but the "doing good" comes naturally; it is a part of "being good."

A person who is not "being good" has a difficult time "doing good" or receiving any enjoyment from it, because it does not come naturally; it is forced. Therefore, it is performed grudgingly or with a selfish desire to receive some reward.

What we are has a tremendous influence upon what we do. Therefore, we need to concern ourselves first with becoming Christ-like and then do our good works for the right reasons, with full purpose of heart.

Consider this conversation:

"Why do you live the commandments?"

"Why? Because I want to enter the celestial kingdom and enjoy eternal life."

"Is that what you really desire?"

"Why certainly; what else?"

What about becoming a better person? What about becoming a "new creature" in Christ (2 Corinthians 5:17), one who reaches out to others in charity, the pure love of Christ? Is that not as important as the reward? And can we really have the reward without first being a better person?

Notice the selfishness in the response to the question "Why do you live the commandments?" Notice the "Because I want . . ."

Where is the pure love of Christ in such an answer? What about charity? The Apostle Paul wrote, "Though I speak with the tongues of men and of angels, and have not charity, I am become as sounding brass, or a tinkling cymbal. And though I have the gift of prophecy, and understand all mysteries, and all knowledge; and though I have all faith, so that I could remove mountains, and have not charity, I am nothing. And though I bestow all my goods to feed the poor, and though I give my body to be burned, and have not charity, it profiteth me nothing." (1 Corinthians 13:1-3.)

Charity "seeketh not her own." (1 Corinthians 13:5.) There is no "because I want" in a charitable person. This may seem hard for us to comprehend, but nevertheless it is true. Not "my will," not "my wants," not "my desires," but "thy will," "thy wants," "thy desires." (See John 5:30.)

When we decide to buckle down and live our religion, we may come up with a list of things we need to do.

The list often looks much like this:

Say my prayers twice a day.

Attend all of my meetings regularly.

Fast every fast Sunday.

Pay an honest tithe.

Attend the temple at least once a month.

Pay a generous fast offering.

Do my home teaching (or visiting teaching).

Read the scriptures daily.

Hold family home evening every Monday.

All these are good works and are essential to spiritual growth. Yet consider the list of one who looks beyond "the law," whose vision has expanded to include not only these works but the spirit behind them. Consider the list of President George Albert Smith:

I would be a friend to the friendless and find joy in ministering to the needs of the poor.

I would visit the sick and afflicted and inspire in them a desire for faith to be healed.

I would teach the truth to the understanding and blessing of all mankind.

I would seek out the erring one and try to win him back to a righteous and happy life.

I would not seek to force people to live up to my ideals, but rather love them into doing the thing that is right.

I would live with the masses and help to solve their problems that their earth life may be happy.

I would avoid the publicity of high positions and discourage the flattery of thoughtless friends.

I would not knowingly wound the feeling of any, not even one who may have wronged me, but would seek to do him good and make him my friend.

I would overcome the tendency to selfishness and jealousy and rejoice in the success of all the children of my Heavenly Father.

I would not be an enemy to any living soul. (In Glen R. Stubbs, "A Biography of George Albert Smith, 1870 to 1951" [Ph.D. diss., Brigham Young University, 1974], p. 440.)

This was his personal, private list. Throughout his list we sense his deep charity. He was following Paul's admonition to "go on to perfection," not by putting aside the necessary guidelines in the first list, but by expanding his vision into the realm of the Spirit.

Were the Apostle Paul alive today, we might very well hear him declare, "Though I say my prayers twice a day, fast once a month, attend all my meetings, and have not charity, I am become as sounding brass, or a tinkling cymbal. And though I pay an honest tithe, attend the temple once a month, hold family home evening, and have not charity, I am nothing. And though I pay a generous fast offering, do my home teaching, and read the scriptures daily, and have not charity, it profiteth me nothing."

Sometimes we want to cry out, "O God, where art thou? How long shall my views be so narrow, my motives so selfish? How long shall I seek glory, dominion, and power, while I neglect my fellowman?

"O God, where art thou? And where is that charity that suffereth long, and is kind; that envieth not, vaunteth not itself, is not puffed up, and doth not behave itself unseemly? Where is that charity that seeketh not her own, is not easily provoked, and thinketh no evil? Where is that charity that rejoiceth not in iniquity but rejoiceth in the truth, which beareth all things, believeth all things, hopeth all things, and endureth all things? O God, where is that charity that never faileth, and how do I obtain it?"

We must seek this Charity above all else, for it is a gift of the Spirit! Let us seek it with full purpose of heart.

Mormon said, "Cleave unto charity, which is the greatest of all, for all things must fail—but charity is the pure love of Christ, and it endureth forever; and whoso is found possessed of it at the last day, it shall be well with him. Wherefore, . . . pray unto the Father with all the energy of heart, that ye may be filled with this love, which he hath bestowed upon all who are true followers of his Son, Jesus Christ; that ye may become the sons of God; that when he shall appear we shall be like him, for we shall see him as he is; that we may have this hope; that we may be purified even as he is pure." (Moroni 7:46-48.)

Living by the Spirit

We think, "Yes, I can change, but how? I want to find God, but where do I start? What must I do that I haven't already done? Where am I going wrong?

George Q. Cannon gave this answer: "There may be souls here hungering for the word of God, tried and tempted in many directions, annoyed and perplexed with the cares of life and with those anxieties that are connected with our earthly existence. Who shall tell these souls that which they need? Can any man out of his own wisdom, from the depths of his own thoughts, give the needed strength and comfort to those hungry souls? It is impossible. *God must do it. God must pour out His Holy Spirit, God must help as he has promised to do, and we His children must put ourselves in a position to be helped so that we can claim the blessing.*" (*Journal of Discourses* 24:179-80; italics added.)

"God must do it . . . and we His children must put ourselves in a position to be helped so that we can claim the blessing." That is the key—a joint effort between us and our Father.

Notice the joint effort that is alluded to in this scripture: "Sanctify yourselves; yea, purify your hearts, and cleanse your hands and your feet before me, that I may make you clean." (D&C 88:74.)

We must put forth a conscientious effort to sanctify ourselves, to purify our hearts, hands, and feet before God. After we have exerted this effort, God performs the spiritual cleansing that was beyond our power to accomplish. How? "God must pour out his Holy Spirit."

And when we are made clean and have the companionship of the Holy Ghost, we will know what works to do and how to conduct our lives.

Nephi said, "I suppose that ye ponder somewhat in your hearts concerning that which ye should do after ye have entered in by the way. But, behold, why do ye ponder these things in your hearts? . . . For behold, . . . I say unto you that if ye will enter in by the way, and receive the Holy Ghost, it will show unto you all things what ye should do." (2 Nephi 32:1, 5.)

On February 23, 1847, Brigham Young recorded:

While sick and asleep about noonday of the 17th inst., I dreamed that I went to see Joseph. He looked perfectly natural, sitting with his feet on the lower round of his chair. I took hold of his right hand and kissed him many times, and said to him: "Why is it that we cannot be together as we used to be, you have been from us a long time, and we want your society and I do not like to be separated from you."

Joseph rising from his chair and looking at me with his usual, earnest, expressive and pleasing countenance replied, "It is all right."

I said, "I do not like to be away from you."

Joseph said, "It is all right; we cannot be together yet; we shall be by and by; but you will have to do without me a while, and then we shall be together again."

I then discovered there was a hand rail between us, Joseph stood by a window and to the southwest of him it was very light. I was in the twilight and to the north of me it was very dark; I said, "Brother Joseph, the brethren you know well, better than I do; you raised them up, and brought the Priesthood to us. The brethren have a great anxiety to understand the law of adoption or sealing principles; and if you have a word of counsel for me I should be glad to receive it."

Joseph stepped toward me, and looking very earnestly, yet pleasantly said, "Tell the people to be humble and faithful, and be sure to keep the spirit of the Lord and it will lead them right. Be careful and not turn away the small still voice; it will teach you what to do and where to go; it will yield the fruits of the kingdom.

"Tell the brethren to keep their hearts open to conviction, so that when the Holy Ghost comes to them, their hearts will be ready to receive it. They can tell the Spirit of the Lord from all other spirits; it will whisper peace and joy to their souls; it will take malice, hatred, strife and all evil from their hearts; and their whole desire will be to do good, bring forth righteousness and build up the kingdom of God. Tell the brethren if they will follow the spirit of the Lord they will go right.

"Be sure to tell the people to keep the Spirit of the Lord; and if they will, they will find themselves just as they were organized by our Father in Heaven before they came into the world. Our Father in Heaven organized the human family, but they are all disorganized and in great confusion."

Joseph then showed me the pattern, how they were in the beginning. This I cannot describe, but I saw it, and saw where the Priesthood had been taken from the earth and how it must be joined together, so that there would be a perfect chain from Father Adam to his latest posterity.

Joseph again said, "Tell the people to be sure to keep the Spirit of the Lord and follow it, and it will lead them just right." (Elden J. Watson, comp., *Manuscript History of Brigham Young 1846-1847*, pp. 528-30.)

Again and again, Joseph Smith reminded Brigham Young to "tell the people to be sure to keep the Spirit of the Lord." What greater message could he convey? What more could he want than for the Saints to have the companionship of the Holy Ghost?

The Prophet Joseph knew that if the Saints would keep the Spirit of the Lord in their hearts and follow its admonitions, it would "lead them right" and they would "go right."

If we are led right and go right, it is because the course we are following is right in the sight of God. As we continue, eventually we will discover that our thoughts, words, and deeds are right, and that the state of our souls is right for celestial inheritance, all because we courted the Spirit of the Lord, followed its admonitions, and let its light grow brighter and brighter until the perfect day.

Bibliography

Journal of Discourses. 26 vols. London: Latter-day Saints' Book Depot, 1854-86.

Smith, Joseph. *Lectures on Faith.* Compiled by N. B. Lundwall. Salt Lake City: N. B. Lundwall, n. d.

———. *Teachings of the Prophet Joseph Smith.* Selected by Joseph Fielding Smith. Salt Lake City: Deseret Book Company, 1938.

Snow, Eliza R. *Biography and Family Record of Lorenzo Snow.* Salt Lake City: Deseret News Company, Printers, 1884.

Stubbs, Glen R. "A Biography of George Albert Smith, 1870 to 1951." Ph.D. diss., Brigham Young University, 1974.

Watson, Elden J., comp. *Manuscript History of Brigham Young, 1846-1847.* Salt Lake City: Elden J. Watson, 1971.

Index